DON'T PLAY FOR THE TIE

BEAR BRYANT ON LIFE

By Creed & Heidi Tyline King

RUTLEDGE HILL PRESS®

Nashville, Tennessee

A Division of Thomas Nelson Publishers
www.ThomasNelson.com

Published by Rutledge Hill Press, a division of Thomas Nelson, Inc., P.O. Box 141000, Nashville, Tennessee 37214.

Rutledge Hill Press books may be purchased in bulk for educational, business, fund-raising, or sales promotional use. For information, please e-mail SpecialMarkets@ThomasNelson.com.

Library of Congress Cataloging-in-Publication Data

Bryant, Paul W.
    Don't play for the tie : Bear Bryant on life / [compiled by] Creed and Heidi Tyline King.
      p. cm.
    Includes bibliographical references.
    ISBN 1-4016-0299-1 (hardcover)
    1. Bryant, Paul W.—Quotations. 2. Football—Quotations, maxims, etc. I. King, Creed, 1965- II. King, Heidi Tyline, 1966- III. Title.
  GV939.B79A3 2006
  796.332—dc22
  2006012606

Printed in the United States of America

06 07 08 09 10 WOR 5 4 3 2 1

FOREWORD

Ihave always loved sports, any sport, and I always knew that I was going to be a sportscaster. As a teenager, I'd leave my home in Brooklyn, take the subway to the Port Authority Bus Terminal, and then ride a Greyhound bus to Pittsburgh, to Montreal, to wherever the games were being played. I just had to be there, to be a part of the action, and calling the action was something that I always knew I wanted to do.

My road to a broadcasting career was tough going at first. I put in my dues first as a peanut vendor at Madison Square Garden, then as a summer relief audio engineer for ABC radio. I was promoted to office boy for the Madison Square Garden Corporation and worked weekends at some of New York City's biggest radio stations. I eventually got a job calling minor league hockey and baseball games. I rode the buses for twelve years broadcasting those games. Those were some tough times, but it also was an invaluable learning experience.

Growing up in Brooklyn, I didn't know college football as a kid. We had the Giants and the Jets. I was a huge sports fan, but I hate to say it, as a kid, I had no idea who Paul "Bear" Bryant was. That is, until the late seventies when I moved to Birmingham to broadcast the minor league hockey team, the Birmingham Bulls. I loved Alabama from the start, the slower pace, the friendly faces, and the open spaces. Before I knew it I was caught up in the fervor that is Alabama football, and I quickly learned who the driving force was behind the Tide: Coach Bryant. I came to respect the man as a legend in his own time. His single-minded devotion and unwavering discipline struck a chord with me. His determination and work ethic reminded me of what it took for me to succeed and inspired me as I continued on my career path.

Indeed, Paul "Bear" Bryant left an enormous legacy that lingers to this day. When he retired as head coach of the University of Alabama's Crimson Tide football team, he was the *winningest* college football coach in history with 323 victories. But as most Bama fans know, the Bear's legacy went beyond producing winning football teams. He left something else in his wake that was an inspiring combination of class, pride, and charisma. This icon—known well to hard core fans and everyday folks as the tough look-ing guy in the houndstooth hat—made a lasting impression on absolutely every person he met. And for those lucky enough to call him coach, his influence was undeniable and ultimately long-lasting.

When I anchored the live, day-long broadcast of Coach Bryant's funeral, I realized what this man meant to the people of Alabama and countless others across the country. Bear Bryant had a lasting influence on players again and again. Just last year, before a New York Jets game, I sat down with Marty Lyons. This former Jets and Alabama star, now a Jets broadcaster, had one thing on his mind—Coach Bryant. That was the topic of our conversation in 2005, almost twenty-five-years after Coach Bryant's death.

He was a great man with much wisdom and influence. His memory will live on forever in the lives that he touched and the example that he set. Let his words of wisdom inspire you today.

INTRODUCTION

Paul "Bear" Bryant, one of the winningest coaches in major college football history, was more than a mastermind at the game. He was a motivator. He believed that hard work, dedication, and self-confidenceæthe traits that rescued him from a life of "plowing and driving those mules and chopping cotton for fifty cents a day". They were the keys to success both on and off the playing field, and he considered it his job to instill such characteristics in his players. "Lessons can be taught in football that are difficult to get across in the home, church, or classroom," he said. "It's my pleasure as a coach to watch a young man apply these lessons later in life."

Bryant was born on September 11, 1913, in Moro Bottom, Arkansas, the eleventh of twelve children. His father was a semi-invalid and as his older brothers left home, Bryant had to shoulder much of the responsibility and chores that came with farming 260 acres. He plowed barefoot, milked cows, chopped cotton, and peddled produce with his mother in nearby Fordyce. His childhood was hard, but it was also happy; one filled with boyish pranks like the shenanigan that earned him his nickname, "Bear." On a bet, the twelve-year-old wrestled a bear. Though Bryant pinned the bear, he never collected his money, but the nickname stuck, and Bryant basked in the attention he received.

Another defining characteristic of his childhood was the devotion and love between mother and son. As a coach, he emphasized to players the importance of keeping in touch, and thought it was healthy for every one of them to "find time to write their mother and go see their mother." Years later, while saying his lines in the now-famous commercial for South Central Bell telephone company, Bryant asked, "Have you called your Mama lately?, then replied impromptu, "I sure wish I could call mine."

While Bryant was ashamed of being poor and embarrassed by the stigmas that it imposed upon him, his childhood ultimately shaped him into the man he would become. His size made him a natural for football, and he used the sport to lift him out of poverty and a life of farming. His father didn't want him to play, but his mother turned her head the other way, and in high school, he became an all-state player. His team, the Fordyce Redbugs, won back-to-back state football championships in 1929 and 1930. Bryant's performance attracted scouts from several colleges; he chose Alabama for the attention—everybody in the South had heard of the

Crimson Tide. Despite failing to graduate with his class, Bryant accepted an athletic scholarship to Alabama. Upon arriving in Tuscaloosa in 1931, he enrolled in high school for the fall semester to earn his degree while practicing with the Crimson Tide.

Bryant lettered for the Tide for three years, and won two conference championships and a national championship in 1934. His most memorable game occurred during his senior year, when he played with a broken leg against Tennessee. The game was among his best, and Bama beat the Volunteers 25–0. It was also as an undergraduate that he met and married Mary Harmon Black, "the best looking gal you or I have ever laid eyes on."

Bryant began his coaching career with a short stint at Union College in Jackson, Tennessee, followed by three years as an assistant coach at Alabama and two years as an assistant at Vanderbilt. When World War II broke out, he enlisted immediately and spent the next four years in the Navy, serving time in North Africa and the North Carolina Pre-Flight Training at C*hapel Hill, where he coached football until the war ended.

After the war, he landed his first job as a head coach with the University of Maryland, turning a team with only one win the season before into a winner with a 6–2–1 record. He left, however, after a year, when the president fired a coach while Bryant was away and reinstated a player that had been kicked off the team. Interferences such as these would not be tolerated by Bryant throughout his career.

Bryant went to the University of Kentucky in 1946 and coached the Wildcats for eight seasons. During his tenure, the Wildcats posted eight consecutive winning seasons, won four bowl games and captured the school's first conference championship in football. He remains, even today, the school's winningest football coach, with sixty wins. No doubt Bryant could have finished his career in Lexington, but the state was primarily basketball country, and Bryant didn't like being in the shadow of basketball coach Adolph Rupp. After a fiercely contested battle, he was allowed to break his contract.

Bryant's next stop was College Station, Texas, home of the Texas A&M Aggies. A&M wasn't his first choice for a new assignment, but it was the only one with a head coach opening suitable for him. During his inaugural (1954) season in College Station, he took the team to Junction City for what proved to be a brutal training camp. His practices were so rigorous that Bryant returned trailed by a bedraggled bunch of misfits who somehow managed to tough it out—including future Crimson Tide Coach Gene Stallings. Bryant's first A&M team struggled to a 1–9 season, but he managed to build winning teams the following three years, including a

Southwest Conference champion in 1956. A year later John David Crow became Bryant's only Heisman Trophy winner.

In 1958, Bryant was named head coach at Alabama. Commenting on his return to his alma mater, Bryant said it was "like when you were out in the field and you heard your mama calling you to dinner. Mama called." It was the beginning of a twenty-five year reign at Bama—one that made him a legend in college football. It also turned him into Alabama's favorite son—so much so that even today, people are still naming their children after Paul "Bear" Bryant.

Bryant's career coaching accomplishments were phenomenal. They included 323 victories, twenty-nine bowl appearances (twenty-four of which were consecutive) in thirty-eight seasons, national coach of the year honors in 1961, 1971, and 1973, six national championships (five Associated Press championships in 1961, 1964, 1965, 1978, 1979 and a separate United Press championship in 1973), two coach-of-the-decade honors, and twenty-five conference titles.

Bryant retired in 1982 after a victory in the Liberty Bowl against Illinois. Shortly after, on January 26, 1983, he passed away. Flags across the state flew at half staff, and a line of fans stretched almost the entire distance from Tuscaloosa to Birmingham, where he was buried.

While football made a name for Bryant, his legacy to the players, coaches, and fans who knew and followed him is the way he turned football into an analogy for life. Today, almost twenty-five years after his death, people across the country continue to use Bryant's words of wisdom as encouragement in their lives. He often said that "Mama wanted me to be a preacher. I told her coachin' and preachin' were a lot alike."

How right he was.

DON'T PLAY FOR THE TIE

When you're number one,
you don't play for the tie.

I'm not interested in moral victories. That's too much like kissing your sister. I'm interested in winning, and all this stuff about building character with a losing team is a bunch of tommyrot.

■ ■ ■

If wanting to win is a fault, as some of my critics seem to insist, then I plead guilty. I like to win. I know no other way. It's in my blood.

There are three types of football players. First, there are those who are winners and know they are winners. Then, there are the losers who know they are losers. Then there are those who are not winners but don't know it. They're the ones for me. They never quit trying. They're the soul of our game.

■ ■ ■

Like I said, though. I don't really consider it a loss. We just ran out of time.

[ON LOSING 24–23 TO NOTRE DAME IN THE 1973 SUGAR BOWL]

Be humble. It's awfully easy for an athlete to get so wrapped up in himself that he doesn't know what's going on around him. I get more publicity than anybody around the university, but there are a lot of people there more important than I am. I think about that every day.

■ ■ ■

It is not an "I" thing, it is a "WE" thing.

[ON WIN NUMBER 315]

■ ■ ■

There's no substitute for guts.

Football changes and so do people. The successful coach is the one who sets the trend, not the one who follows it.

■ ■ ■

Don't over-coach them. Let them play some. If you're out there coaching them all the time, when are they going to practice?

■ ■ ■

When I was a young coach I used to say, "Treat everybody alike." That's bull. Treat everybody fairly.

I still get up at five o'clock.
I'd like to sleep later but after
thirty-seven years in this business
I find I can't. To me it's still time
wasted when you sleep past six.

Be yourself. Don't try to copy anyone else.

■ ■ ■

I don't hire anybody not brighter than I am. If they're not smarter than me, I don't need them.

■ ■ ■

I don't make a lot of rules for my players. I expect them to act like gentlemen, to have good table manners, to be punctual, to be prayerful. I expect them to be up on their studies, and I don't expect them to be mooning around the campus holding hands with the girls all the time, because that comes later, when they're winners.

Winning isn't imperative, but coming from behind and getting tougher in the fourth quarter is. I don't want you to think you have to win, because you don't. On the other hand, if you can go out there ripping and snorting and having fun by knocking people around, I assure you—you will win!

■ ■ ■

Smile. You'll catch a lot more bugs if you smile than you will with vinegar or something.

Photo courtesy of the Paul W. Bryant Museum, the University of Alabama.

Bear Bryant at the taping of a Bob Hope TV special in the 1980s

After the game there are three types of people. One comes in and he ain't played worth killing, and he's lost. And he gets dressed and out of there as quick as he can. He meets his girl and his mama, and they ain't too damn glad to see him. And he goes off somewhere and says how "the coach shoulda done this or that," and "the coach don't like me," and "I didn't play enough." And everybody just nods. And the second type will sit there a while, thinking what he could have done to make his team a winner. And he'll shed some tears. He'll finally get dressed, but he doesn't want to see anybody. His mama's out there. She puts on a big act and tells him what a great game he played, and he tells her if he had done this or that he'd be a winner, and that he will be a winner—next week. And then there's the third guy. The winner. He'll be in there hugging everybody in the dressing room. It'll take him an hour to dress. And when he goes out it's a little something extra in it when his daddy squeezes his hand. His mama hugs and kisses him, and that little old ugly girl snuggles up, proud to be next to him. And he knows they're proud. And why.

Joe Namath and Coach Bryant had mutual respect and admiration.

His nickname was Bear.

Now imagine a guy that can

carry the nickname Bear.

JOE NAMATH on ESPN Classic's SportsCentury series.

There is no sin in not liking to play; it's a mistake for a boy to be there if he doesn't want to.

■ ■ ■

I tell all my coaches you have to have a plan for everything, an objective, you just don't go out day-to-day and coach. You have a plan you believe in and you have to be strong enough not to compromise.

■ ■ ■

There is a big difference in wanting to and willing to.

Every man I had left on the [Junction Boys] team felt he could whip Joe Louis on Saturday. The difference between winning and losing is attitude.

■ ■ ■

I think the most important thing of all for any team is a winning attitude. The coaches must have it. The players must have it. The student body must have it. If you have dedicated players who believe in themselves, you don't need a lot of talent.

■ ■ ■

You don't strive for sameness, you strive for balance.

Over the years I've learned a lot about coaching staffs, and the one piece of advice I would pass on to a young head coach, or a corporation executive, or even a bank president is this: don't make them in your image. Don't even try. My assistants don't look alike, think alike, or have the same personalities. And I sure don't want them all thinking like I do.

■ ■ ■

You're never too old until you think you are.

If you don't have discipline, you can't have a successful program.

■ ■ ■

It's a lot better to be seen than heard. The sun is the most powerful thing I know of and it doesn't make much noise.

■ ■ ■

I'm not much of a golfer, I don't have any friends, and all I like to do is go home and be alone, and *not* worry about ways not to lose.

I'm just a plowhand from Arkansas, but
I have learned over the years how to hold a
team together—how to lift some men up,
how to calm down others, until finally
they've got one heartbeat, together, a team.

Coach Bryant on the Quad at the University of Alabama

As long as you know within yourself—and the guys with you know it—that you have confidence in the plan, you know you are not going to fail.

■ ■ ■

The one that makes you proud is the one who isn't good enough to play, but it means so much to him, he puts so much into it, that he plays anyway.

■ ■ ■

Find the talent and relate to it.

The idea of molding men means a lot to me.

■ ■ ■

I have tried to teach them to show class, to have pride and to display character. I think football, winning games, takes care of itself if you do that.

■ ■ ■

They *think* they're good enough to win, and they go out and win.

Don't change your game plan unless
you have to. Certainly, you've got to
have a plan that's flexible. Don't
change when it isn't necessary.

In a crisis, don't hide behind anything or anybody. They're going to find you anyway.

■ ■ ■

As far as the critics, well, they don't know what the hell they're talking about. Most of them have ridden their daddies' coattails and haven't done a thing on their own anyway.

What we gotta do is suck our own guts up—not depend on someone else to lose theirs.

■ ■ ■

Don't give up. Reach down inside of you and you'll find something left.

■ ■ ■

It's an old story. You stick your head above the crowd and you're going to have people trying to knock it off.

Losing doesn't make me want
to quit. It makes me want to
fight that much harder.

Some coaches have accused me of being too defense-minded, but most of those who said that have wound up being athletic directors.

■ ■ ■

If you start to make a decision, go ahead and make it. Don't mealy-mouth around.

If you're caught with a weak team, don't try to get fancy and please the spectators. The weaker you are, the more conservatively you must play. You play that way and you might win. At least you'll be respectable.

■ ■ ■

I'm no miracle man. I guarantee nothing but hard work.

Do things you don't like to do,
bear down that much harder
on what you hate doing. It'll
make you a lot better player.
And a lot better person.

I'll never give up on a player regardless of his ability as long as he never gives up on himself. In time he will develop.

■ ■ ■

It's still a coach's game. Make no mistake. You start at the top. If you don't have a good one at the top, you don't have a cut dog's chance. If you do, the rest falls into place. You have to have good assistants, and a lot of things, but first you have to have the chairman of the board. Then you have to recruit, and then you have to get them to play.

Stay organized and keep things simple.

■ ■ ■

You're still going to win with preparation and dedication and plain old desire. If you don't have genuine desire, you won't be dedicated enough to prepare properly.

■ ■ ■

Formations don't win football games, people do. But they can give you an edge, and that's what coaches look for. That's why we change so much.

A coach is stupid if he doesn't do what is best for his people.

■ ■ ■

I don't try to save the world. I just go at it one football player at a time.

■ ■ ■

I remember so well, after I played my last game, how alone I felt, and I want my boys to always feel they can come to me. And I'll say this, you can learn as much from them as you can teach them.

Paul Bryant and Joe Paterno mixing punch at a Sugar Bowl Banquet

Photo courtesy of the Paul W. Bryant Museum, the University of Alabama.

Even his peers in the coaching business
felt in awe of him. He had such
charisma. He was just a giant figure.

JOE PATERNO, head coach for Penn State

Is work fun? I love to go to practice; I get a thrill every time I walk on that field. I thank the good Lord every day I walk on that field. I get a big letdown after the game is over. After the bowl game, it takes two to three days for it to sink in that the season is over.

■ ■ ■

Put everything you've got into anything you do.

The first time you quit, it's hard. The second time, it gets easier. The third time, you don't even have to think about it.

■ ■ ■

Don't give up on yourself. How you do this fall will go a long way in shaping your life, and don't you ever doubt it.

[TALK TO INCOMING PLAYERS]

I tell young players who want to be coaches, who think they can put up with all the headaches and heartaches, "Can you live without it? If you can live without it, don't get in it."

■ ■ ■

Don't give up before the game starts. I lost a Kentucky game with Georgia in 1946 simply because I didn't believe we could win.

■ ■ ■

A quick, small team can beat a big, slow team any time.

There's no easy way to win, and
the tougher it is the more they have
to believe in you, and to trust you.

If my 75 percent boy plays 15 percent over his ability and your 100 percent boy slogs around and plays 15 percent under his, then we will beat you every time.

■ ■ ■

You don't win those things [championships] in that last game against Auburn and you don't win 'em in a bowl. They are won in August and early September, maybe even before that, in the summer, when the players are still at home.

If you believe in yourself and have dedication and pride, and never quit, you'll be a winner. The price of victory is high but so are the rewards.

■　■　■

If you get ahead then play like you're behind.

■　■　■

Don't ruin a practice by not disciplining yourself. If you're upset, don't take it out on your team.

Have a goal. And to reach that goal, you'd better have a plan. Have a plan that you believe in so strongly you'll never compromise.

Be good or be gone.

[SIGN IN BEAR'S OFFICE AT KENTUCKY]

■ ■ ■

Win or lose, if you don't recognize the mistakes—mistakes in preparation, mistakes during a game—you're hurting yourself. I've been outcoached, too, and I sure don't forget those times. Do they live as long as the big victories? No. They live longer.

Coach Bryant watching warm-ups before a game

If they don't have a winning attitude, I don't want them.

■ ■ ■

I'm not saying we'll win *any* games, but I will say that the only thing that will satisfy us is to win twelve.

■ ■ ■

The ones who have ability and don't use it are the ones who eat your guts out. I've messed up my share of those.

I'm not trying to tell you I told you so, but I'll tell you like I always try to tell you and like any coach will tell you—ten minutes after the game, it's too late. The next day is too late. So the best thing we can do is to use this as a stepping-stone, and if we've got class—we'll be all right. If we haven't, then it doesn't matter, does it?

■ ■ ■

I'm not as smart as other coaches; I have to work harder.

[WHEN ASKED WHEY HE HAD TO GET UP AT FIVE O'CLOCK IN THE MORNING]

Success in anything is a matter of timing, no matter what
you do.

■ ■ ■

Set goals, high goals, for you and your organization.
When your organization has a goal to shoot for, you
create teamwork, people working for a common good.
Teamwork is imperative. Don't forget that. People who
are in it for their own good are individualists. They don't
share the same heartbeat that makes a team so great. A
great unit, whether it be football or any organization,
shares the same heartbeat.

His name is still as powerful and strong
as ever to me. He had it all. I've been around
a lot of big-name coaches. None of them
have the presence of Coach Bryant. When the
man walked in a room, everyone watched
him. . . . I think from 1968 on, everybody
who ran for president came to see
him. That's the kind of clout he had.
He just attracted people to him.

MAL MOORE, athletic director for Alabama and former player

The same things win today that have always won, and they will win years from now. The only difference is the losers have a whole new bunch of excuses why they don't win or can't win.

■ ■ ■

We can't have two standards, one set for the dedicated young men who want to do something ambitious, and one set for those who don't.

Have a plan in your life and be
able to adjust it. Have a plan when
you wake up, what you're going
to do with your day. Just don't
go lollygagging through any day
of your life. I hope I have had
some luck in my life because I
have planned for the good
times and the bad ones.

We're on a longer road. We've got a bigger [game] next week, and the week after. Because the next game is always more important if you're going to the top. And that's where we're going.

■ ■ ■

You've got to keep from losing before you can win. There is a difference between losing and getting beat. There is a difference between winning and beating people. If we keep from losing, the worst we'll come out with is a tie.

When you can't score from the 1 [yard line], you don't deserve to win.

■ ■ ■

Keep your head up; act like a champion.

■ ■ ■

I don't have any ideas, my coaches have them. I just pass the ideas on and referee the arguments.

Photo courtesy of the Paul W. Bryant Museum, the University of Alabama.

Bear Bryant at the 1980 Sugar Bowl where he beat Lou Holtz Arkansas Razorbacks 24–9

It's awfully important to win with humility. It's also important to lose. I hate to lose worse than anyone, but if you never lose you won't know how to act. If you lose with humility, then you can come back.

■ ■ ■

Sure, being hungry could be a great motivator, but coaching is a lot more fun if you don't have to do it for a living.

Don't overwork your squad. If you're going to make a mistake, under-work them.

■ ■ ■

As long as I'm right, I don't give a damn what people think.

■ ■ ■

I'm no innovator. If anything I'm a stealer, or borrower. I've stolen or borrowed from more people than you can shake a stick at.

Work hard. There is no substitute for hard work. None. If you work hard, the folks around you are going to work harder.

You learn to work. You have to work hard to succeed in anything.

■ ■ ■

I don't want ideas just thrown out, I want them *thought* out.

■ ■ ■

Football has been a road out of poverty for many a young man. When you don't have anything to go back to, then by gosh you're going to work a little harder.

Listen, does your boy know how to work? Try to teach him to work, to sacrifice, to fight. He better learn now, because he's going to have to do it someday. I mean, some morning when you've been out of school twenty years and you wake up and your house has burned down and your mother is in the hospital and the kids are all sick and you're overdrawn at the bank and your wife has run off with the drummer, what are you going to do? Throw in?

Make something happen.

■ ■ ■

Nothing happens by accident. You make your own luck.

■ ■ ■

I don't know what class is, but I can tell when one has it. You can tell it from a mile away.

When you make a mistake, there are only three things you should ever do about it: admit it; learn from it; and don't repeat it.

■ ■ ■

If a man is a quitter, I'd rather find out in practice than in a game. I ask for all a player has so I'll know later what I can expect. Because of that, we probably don't have as much fun during the week as some teams but we have more pleasant Saturdays than most.

He wasn't afraid of what people thought
and said. If anything, I try to do like him,
I don't let public opinion tell me what to do.

BOBBY BOWDEN, head coach for Florida State

You never know how a
horse will pull until you hook
him to a heavy load.

I always want my players to show class, knock 'em down, pat them on the back, and run back to the huddle.

■ ■ ■

Keep your poise.

■ ■ ■

Never compromise with what you think is right.

■ ■ ■

Don't talk too much or too soon.

Don't do a lot of coaching just before the game. If you haven't coached them by fourteen minutes to two on Saturday, it's too late then.

■ ■ ■

Leaders are self-starters. They say, "let's go" and lead. They don't say "sic 'em" and step back to watch the fighters do the work.

You don't have to talk a lot to be a leader. Lee Roy Jordan was a great leader, and he never said a word. But if he grunted, everybody listened.

■ ■ ■

The thing about recruiting is that you have to learn—and learn fast—that you can't make the chicken salad without the chicken.

You can't throw a fit once a month, go down and shake somebody, and impress him very much. They think, who the hell is this? You're like a shower coming down: just wait and it goes away. If you're in the trenches with them every day, they'll do anything you want.

■ ■ ■

Recognize winners. (They come in all sizes, colors, shapes.) Get the winners into the game.

Learn from others. Ask questions.
Be a good listener. Get a pulse beat
of what is going on around you.

Little things make me proud.

■ ■ ■

I think anyone is wrong to get involved in one thing so completely all his life like I have. You get to a point when thirty minutes after the last game you start thinking about the next one. That's not all there is in life.

I have let football rob me of some valuable time that I should have been spending with [my wife] and with my daughter and my son.

■ ■ ■

I've always tried to stress to my players that they need to grow each day of their life in three important ways: mentally, physically, and spiritually. If they'd do that, they'll be all right.

Always be totally loyal to your staff. If you are, then they'll be loyal back. Remember, loyalty and honesty are two-way streets. If you are ever dishonest to members of your staff, you'll never regain their respect.

■ ■ ■

Age has nothing to do with it. You can be out of touch at any age.

At graduation where Paul Bryant received an honorary Doctor of Laws degree

In a way, it was a nightmare. The team had very little ability, but my, what character! They could have given up a hundred times—but they didn't. And I firmly believe that, if I had done a better job, we wouldn't have lost at Texas A&M.

■ ■ ■

Bigness is in the heart.

Today we Americans lost a hero who always
seemed larger than life. . . . Bear Bryant
gave his country the gift of a life unsurpassed.
In making the impossible seem easy,
he lived what we strive to be.

President Ronald Reagan

If there is one thing that has helped me as a coach, it's my ability to recognize winners, or good people who can become winners by paying a price.

■ ■ ■

Always be totally loyal to the institution for which you work. If you don't have the best interest of the organization at heart or if you can't be loyal, you are in the wrong place.

■ ■ ■

I can reach a kid who doesn't have any ability as long as he doesn't know it.

Photo courtesy of the Paul W. Bryant Museum, the University of Alabama.

Bryant at a taping of a Bob Hope TV special in the 1980s

Everybody is different. If you treat them all alike you won't reach them. Be fair with all of them and you have a chance. One you pat on the back and he'll jump out the window for you. Another you kick in the tail. A third you yell at and squeeze a little. But be fair. And that's what I am.

■ ■ ■

Motivating people is the ingredient that separates winners from losers.

The old lessons (work, self-discipline, sacrifice, teamwork, fighting to achieve) aren't being taught by many people other than football coaches these days. The football coach has a captive audience and can teach these lessons because the communication lines between himself and his players are more wide open than between kids and [their] parents.

■ ■ ■

If a person doesn't help himself—if he isn't accountable for his own mistakes or oversights—he shouldn't expect others to help him either.

When I correct them in a meeting it's always "we" or "our" mistake, so they know it's a team deal, that we're responsible as a team. If I have to criticize, I like to start with something positive. Then when I've got their attention—they're always going to agree with you when you're telling 'em something good—I come back and say, "But boys, we are covering kickoffs like we're trying to live forever."

■ ■ ■

I'm not sure we beat them, but we won. That's good enough.

Steve Wright, the only man to play for both
Vince Lombardi and Bryant, once told me
that playing for Bryant was "like having
John Wayne for your grandfather."

ALLEN BARRA, author and columnist

Certainly [football] is still challenging—not the game itself, but the preparation, the planning, the practice, and of course, the recruiting. However, the real challenge is creating a winning attitude in the players. The kind of feeling you can create on the practice field, the atmosphere around the dorm, these are the things that determine what kind of game you'll have.

■ ■ ■

Communication. It's the key to everything. You *have* to have it to win, and when you *lose*, too, so you can hold them in your hand.

Paul "Bear" Bryant

Photo courtesy of the Paul W. Bryant Museum, the University of Alabama.

On the field I try not to make any decisions unless they have particular significance—I don't mean I sit there on my fat fanny, like I have done in some games, thinking or praying they would do it when I knew I should have— but I try to have a plan and the guts to stick to it no matter what happens.

■ ■ ■

I've made so many mistakes that if I don't make the same mistakes over, we're going to come pretty close to winning.

In life, you'll have your back up against the wall many times. You might as well get used to it.

I've never had any complaints on winning.

■ ■ ■

We've been able to do more with ordinary players because we don't tell them they are ordinary. Our best teams usually had four or five great players and a lot of average ones.

■ ■ ■

You take those little rascals, talk to them good, pat them on the back, let them think they are good, and they will go out and beat the big 'uns.

If you whoop and holler all the time the players just get used to it.

■ ■ ■

I know what it takes to win. If I can sell them on what it takes to win, then we are not going to lose too many football games.

■ ■ ■

Coming from behind is still one of the greatest lessons, and the ability to do it is the mark of a great team.

If you get knocked down, get up.

■ ■ ■

I have always tried to teach my players to be fighters. When I say that, I don't mean put up your dukes and get in a fistfight over something. I'm talking about facing adversity in your life. There is not a person alive who isn't going to have some awfully bad days in their lives . . . Most people just lay down and quit. Well, I want my people to fight back. Don't quit. I just hope a few of them learned that over the years, and I think they have.

You're never beaten until the clock runs out.

■ ■ ■

Be aware of yes-men. Generally, they are losers. Surround yourself with winners. Never forget: people win. Get people who work for your organization because it means something to them. Most organizations get people who are interested in drawing their paycheck for their forty-hour week. Don't forget, those folks usually don't work but about ten hours out of the forty they are paid for. To be the best—if you want to be the best—get people who care about your institution, people who are proud to be associated with your organization. Get winning people.

There's one thing about quitters you have to guard against: they are contagious. If one boy goes, the chances are he'll take somebody with him, and you don't want that. So when they would start acting that way I used to pack them up and get them out, or embarrass them, or do something to turn them around.

■ ■ ■

Don't ever give up on ability. Don't give up on a player who has it.

When you're teaching a boy to work for the first time in his life and teaching him to sacrifice and suck up his guts when he's behind, which are lessons he has to learn sooner or later, you are going to find boys who are not willing to pay the price.

■ ■ ■

I've told you a jillion times—the defenses or the coaches don't have anything to do with it really—it's the *people* that play!

Players can be divided, roughly, into four types. Those who have ability and know it, those who have it and don't know it, those who don't have it and know it, and those who don't have it but don't know it.

■ ■ ■

Every time a player goes out there, at least twenty people have some amount of influence on him. His mother has more influence than anyone. I know because I played, and I loved my mama.

Photo courtesy of the Paul W. Bryant Museum, the University of Alabama.

In 1934 Paul W. Bryant played as an end for the University of Alabama.

You don't change people's thinking overnight.

■ ■ ■

Have a plan, not only for the day, but for the week and the month and the year and ten years from now. Anticipate. Plan. Anticipate every situation that could arise. Plan for every situation that could arise. Don't think second-by-second on what needs to be done. Have a plan. Follow the plan, and you'll be surprised how successful you can be. Most people don't plan. That's why it is easy to beat most folks.

Find your own picture, your own self in anything that goes bad. It's awfully easy to mouth off at your staff or chew out players, but if it's bad, and you're the head coach, you're responsible. If we have an intercepted pass, I threw it. I'm the head coach. If we get a punt blocked, I caused it. A bad practice, a bad game, it's up to the head coach to assume his responsibility.

■ ■ ■

You try to make your team do something they're not capable of and you get murdered.

There's nobody around (in college football) like that now. I have been around some very strong men, a lot of them, like Gene Stallings and John David Crow. I'm talking about guys who in their own right are almost legends themselves and yet they were all humbled in his presence. That's just how powerful a man he was and how respected he was. Business leaders, I have seen him walk into a room and a hush fell. You just don't see that any more, the respect that he earned from anybody in his presence was truly unbelievable.

SYLVESTER CROOM, head coach for Mississippi State

I always had a plan I believed in so strongly that I thought it would win at Vassar College. I never doubted winning. It was just a question of how long it would take.

■ ■ ■

If you want to coach you have three rules to follow to win. One, surround yourself with people who can't live without football. I've had a lot of them. Two, be able to recognize winners. They come in all forms. And, three, have a plan for everything. A plan for practice, a plan for the game. A plan for being ahead, and a plan for being behind 20–0 at the half with your quarterback hurt.

In terms of hours on the job, at Kentucky and Texas A&M and those first few years at Alabama, I would say it took every hour other than about the three in a twenty-four-hour day. The other three I just wasted. Taking a little nap.

■ ■ ■

It's not the will to win that matters—everyone has that. It's the will to prepare to win that matters.

Techniques alone don't win.

■ ■ ■

The biggest mistake coaches make is taking borderline cases and trying to save them. I'm not talking about grades now, I'm talking about character. I want to know before a boy enrolls about his home life, and what his parents want him to be. And I want him to know the criterion at Alabama is up on my office wall in those four-color pictures.

[REFERRING TO CHAMPIONSHIP PHOTOGRAPHS]

If a man has the right attitude, even if he is average, he'll work hard enough to play well. As long as he thinks he can be good, that's all that counts.

■ ■ ■

What better way is there to build character, to instill pride, than to win?

■ ■ ■

Remember you are representing a lot of people—your family, your school, your friends.

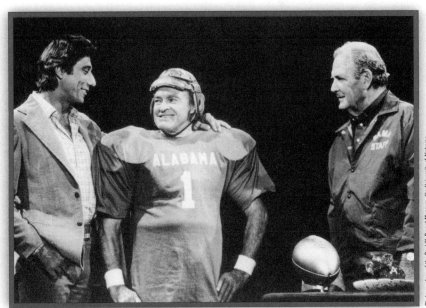

Joe Namath, Bob Hope, and Bear Bryant at the taping of a Bob Hope TV special

Photo courtesy of the Paul W. Bryant Museum, the University of Alabama.

Don't tolerate lazy people. They are losers. People who come to work and watch clocks and pass off responsibilities will only drag you and your organization down. I despise clock-watchers. They don't want to be part of a winning situation. They won't roll up their sleeves when you need them to. If you have lazy people, get rid of them. Remember, it is easy to develop the bad habits of lazy people.

■ ■ ■

You have to be willing to out-condition your opponents.

Don't look back, don't lose your guts, and teach your team to go out on the field and make things happen.

■ ■ ■

I was going to get in the first lick. That's the most important one. There might not be a second.

[SPEAKING ABOUT A FIGHT HE GOT INTO IN HIGH SCHOOL]

Don't get fancy. Every time you think you weaken the team. Hit 'em! Show me some barnyard football.

■ ■ ■

Little things make the difference. Everyone is well-prepared in the big things but only the winners perfect the little things.

■ ■ ■

Scout yourself. Have a buddy who coaches scout you.

I tell my players they're special. They're something everybody should be proud of. They're not like the other students. I say, "If you were we'd have 15,000 out for football. You've got to take pride in being something special."

■ ■ ■

I want a player with pride and one that knows what it takes to excel.

If you played for Bryant, to this day,
you belong in a special group. I have met
old guys who played for him at Kentucky
and I never met them before and let me tell
you something, it's a calling card. If
someone played for Coach Bryant, you
immediately respected the guy.

SYLVESTER CROOM, head coach for Mississippi State

Never quit. It is the easiest cop-out in the world. Set a goal and don't quit until you attain it. When you do attain it, set another goal and don't quit until you reach it. Never quit.

■ ■ ■

Don't worry about winning personality contests with your staff. You'd better worry about being respected. Anybody can be liked, a heck of a lot fewer respected.

I think a boy respects you more when you show him you're willing to sacrifice as much as you want him to.

■ ■ ■

I believe if you have rules you abide by them.

■ ■ ■

Everybody—and I mean coaches, players, managers, everybody—has to suck 'em up and work and scratch and pray and fight to win.

Sacrifice. I don't think anyone can go to school, do well academically and athletically and do all the things other people do. You have to pass up a few things, not because I say so but because you have enough pride.

■ ■ ■

My attitude has always been . . . if it's worth playing, it's worth paying the price to win.

Don't lose your game at the half. Concentrate on winning in the second half. Don't waste time on stuff that can't help you.

■ ■ ■

Play 'em jaw to jaw, and you'll win in the fourth quarter.

■ ■ ■

There's a lot of blood, sweat, and guts between dreams and success.

Remember, do your job for just six seconds, every play, and make something happen. Don't wait for it to happen. Make it happen. Do that, and we're going to win.

■ ■ ■

Intangibles. I can't even spell intangible, but I know you have to have it. When one man opens a business and goes broke and another man comes behind him and is a success with exactly the same business, that's intangibles.

I want every one of you gentlemen to come by me on your way out, and shake hands and look in that mirror, because when you come back in here tonight you're going to look in it again. You'll have to decide then if you gave your best. And every morning you shave from now on you're going to think about giving your best, because I'm going to make you [think about it]. I'm going to be reminding you.

[PEP TALK TO AN A&M TEAM]

Photo courtesy of the Paul W. Bryant Museum, the University of Alabama.

Just before a game in the late 1970s

Point out to them that they don't have to win, but there is a great difference in the reward from winning than in losing. A game that cannot be played over has to be lived with for life. Point out that only special people win consistently. There is very little difference in being average and being a champion.

■ ■ ■

If you don't have the talent to win with talent alone, you have to compensate.

The thing I try to encourage in our players is to never give up on themselves. I've had some that I've given up on, but they didn't give up on themselves and they came through.

■ ■ ■

Winners [know how to relate to people]. I don't know whether it's knowledge or not. It's just something God gave some but didn't give to others. Some people are able to get along with people and organize this, that, and the other. Some are able to fly, swim, dive. Heck, I can't even swim.

The best coaches, most coaches I've known, weren't Phi Beta Kappa in the classroom.

■ ■ ■

When folks are ignorant you don't condemn them, you teach 'em.

■ ■ ■

Sacrifice. Work. Self-discipline. I teach these things, and my boys don't forget them when they leave.

No coach has ever won a game by what he knows; it's what his players know that counts.

■ ■ ■

The main thing is getting the material and teaching your kids to forget a losing complex. Teach them to *win*.

■ ■ ■

Kids are different, and you want different personalities around them. They can't all relate to one type. On the coaching end, there are blackboard coaches and there are field coaches, and a rare few who are both. With some it's not how much they *know* but how much they can *teach*.

We want our people to be something special.

■ ■ ■

One man doesn't make a team. It takes eleven.

■ ■ ■

In order to have a winner, the team must have a feeling of unity; every player must put the team first—ahead of personal glory.

I told them my system was based on the "ant plan," that I'd gotten the idea watching a colony of ants in Africa during the war. A whole bunch of ants working toward a common goal.

[COMMENTING ON HIS SYSTEM THAT SHOOK UP THE SOUTHWEST CONFERENCE DURING HIS YEARS AT A&M]

■ ■ ■

If anything goes bad, *I* did it. If anything goes semi-good, *we* did it. If anything goes really good, then *you* did it. That's all it takes to get people to win football games for you.

Teamwork . . . oneness, as I like to call it. I don't think there has ever been a self-made man. I think it takes a team.

■ ■ ■

Team victory is more important than individual victory.

■ ■ ■

Winning isn't everything, but it sure beats anything that comes in second.

Common sense tells you the other guy will get careless, get sluggish mentally, and you'll beat him in the fourth quarter because you'll be alert for sudden changes, for blocked kicks and fumbles.

■ ■ ■

You go into your boss's office to ask for a raise, the timing better be right. You walk into the kitchen and give your wife a smack [on the lips]. Sometimes it's just the thing to do, and she eats it up. Other times it don't mean a thing. You might as well kiss the refrigerator.

When we're not in the running for number one, people know I haven't done my job.

■ ■ ■

I honestly believe that if you are willing to out-condition the opponent, have confidence in your ability, be more aggressive than your opponent and have a genuine desire for team victory, you will become the national champions. If you have all the above, you will acquire confidence and poise and you will have those intangibles that win the close ones.

Coach Thomas knew what to say and when to say it, and that's the secret. Timing is everything.

[COACH THOMAS WAS BRYANT'S COACH IN COLLEGE.]

■ ■ ■

Most games are won on five or seven plays. The team that makes the big play wins the game. Lay it on the line every play. Never know which play is the big play. Try to win on this play. When you get eleven people trying to win on every play, you'll win.

A great performer can give a great performance and lose. A great player will do the things it takes to win.

■ ■ ■

If you don't at least try to win you don't deserve the championship.

■ ■ ■

Show class, have pride, and display character. If you do, winning takes care of itself.

I don't know if I'm smart enough to know how to describe a winner, but I guess I've been wise enough or maybe just lucky enough of being able to spot one. I know a winner has dedication and pride and the will to win, and he'll do a little bit extra every day to improve himself and his team. A winner is worried about his team and his school, and he'll outwork people, and he'll sacrifice.

■ ■ ■

We betray our people if we fail to demand a winning attitude and the full cooperation of all concerned in all areas.

You can learn from anybody.

■ ■ ■

There are a lot of lessons in football that are very difficult to teach in the home, in the church, or in the classroom. They're easy to teach on the football field, and if the players don't learn these lessons, then football is not very worthwhile. The lessons are simple: first of all there's work and sacrifice; you have to do a lot of that. Then, there's discipline. Then comes teamwork and cooperation. I've read a lot about successful men. They don't do it alone. It always takes a team.

If you don't learn *anything* but self-discipline, then athletics is worthwhile.

■ ■ ■

What happens today you'll have to live with the rest of the way. You can't get it back if you don't win. It's sixty minutes and over. The losers are the ones who say, 'Oh, I wish I could play it again.' You can't play it again.

The coach, the man, the legend

Set a goal, adopt a plan that will help you to achieve the goal. Chances of things happening in this world without goals are slim. Make sure that the goal means a lot to you. Believe in your plan and don't compromise. Believe that the plan is going to win. Tie to people who believe in the plan. Make sure that your plan makes the player a better person. If it doesn't, you're just using people and the plan can't be worth much.

BIBLIOGRAPHY

Barra, Allen, *The Last Coach*, Norton, 2005.

Bryant, Bear, *Young Athlete.* October, 1980.

Bowden, Bobby, *St. Petersburg Times,* http://www.sptimes.com/News/122801/Sports/Bowden_still_in_awe_o.shtml, December 28, 2001.

Bryant, Paul W., "Thirty Thoughts on an Airplane About Coaching the Game of Football." Speech at National High School Athletic Coaches' Association Convention. Colorado Springs, CO, 1972.

Bryant, Paul W., "Be Proud: Crimson Tide's Dr. Bryant Gives His Recipe for Living at MA Banquet"; Phillip Marshall, *Montgomery Advertiser.*

Bryant, Paul and John Underwood, *Bear: The Hard Life and Good Times of Alabama's Coach Bryant.* Boston and Toronto: Little, Brown and Company (Sports Illustrated Books), 1972.

Bryant, Paul W. and John Underwood. *Bear: The Hard Life and Good Times of Alabama's Coach Bryant.* Little, Brown: New York, 1974.

Bynum, Mike, *Bryant: The Man, the Myth.* Atlanta: Cross Roads Books, 1979.

Croom, Sylvester. *Florida Today*, http://www.floridatoday.com/apps/pbcs.dll/article?AID=/20050927/SPORTS/509270335/1002, September 27, 2005.

Dunnavant, Keith, *Coach.* New York: Simon and Schuster, 1996.

Elebash, Camille, "Bear Bryant." *Sky*, October, 1977, p. 42.

Frady, Marshall, "The Bear in Winter," *Sport*. September, 1975, p. 65.

Freeman, Criswell, *The Wisdom of Southern Football: Common Sense and Uncommon Genius from 101 Gridiron Greats*. Nashville: Walnut Grove Press, 1995.

Langford George, *The Crimson Tide, Alabama Football*. Chicago: Harry Regency Company, 1974.

Maikovich, Andrew J., *Sports Quotations: Maxims, Quips and Pronouncements for Writers and Fans*. Jefferson, N.C. & London: McFarland & Company, Inc. Publishers, 1984.

Maisel, Ivan, "The Bear." *Don Heinrich's College Football*, 1991, p. 9.

Marshall, Benny, *Winning Isn't Everything, But it Beats Anything That Comes in Second*. Nashville: Parthenon Press, 1983.

McKenzie, Mike, "The Bear: a Paradoxical Legend." *Memphis Press-Scimitar*, December 17, 1976 (reprinted from *Tuscaloosa News*).

Moore, Mal, *Dallas Morning News*, http://www.dallasnews.com /sharedcontent/dws/spt/colleges/cottonbowl/stories /122705dnspobamalede.d74caba.html, December 26, 2005.

Peterson, James A. and Bill Cromartie, *Bear Bryant: Countdown to Glory*. New York: Leisure Press, 1983.

Reagan, Ronald, *The Washington Times*, http://www.washtimes.com /sports/20060123-114343-6638r_page2.htm, January 24, 2006.

Reed, Delbert, *Paul "Bear" Bryant: What Made Him A Winner.* Tuscaloosa: Visions Press, 1995.

Reflections, compiled by Bill Lumpkin, January 25, 1993.

Remembering Bear: The Life of Coach Paul "Bear" Bryant, 1913–1983. Birmingham: *Birmingham News,* 1983.

Schoor, Gene, *100 Years of Alabama Football.* Atlanta: Longstreet Press, 1991.

Smith, E. S., *Bear Bryant: Football's Winning Coach.* New York: Walker and Co., 1984.

Stallings, Gene, *Bear Bryant on Winning Football.* Prentice Hall, Englewood, NJ, 1983. (originally published as Building a Championship Football Team, 1960).

Stoddard, Tom, *Turnaround: The Untold Story of Bear Bryant's First Year as Head Coach at Alabama.* Montgomery: Black Belt Press, 1996.

Sugar, Bert Randoph, *The Book of Sports Quotes. A Treasury of the Most Outrageous Wit and Wisdom from Ali to Zimmer.* New York: Quick Fox; Music Sales Corp.,1979.

Woodley, Richard, *The Bear.* New York: Pocket Books, 1984.